Heifetz Collection

PAGANINI
24 Caprices, Op. 1

URTEXT EDITION
Edited by Endre Granat

KEISER®

PREFACE

*Paganini's Musical Style, Instruments,
and Background of this Edition*

NICCOLO PAGANINI (b. 1782, Genoa—d. 1840, Nice), violin virtuoso and composer, revolutionized violin technique by introducing new ways to tune the violin, use harmonics, pizzicato and methods of fingering. He inspired the mystique of the performer and became the first popular star of classical music.

Paganini's favorite violin was built by Giuseppe Guarneri del Gesù in 1743. He named this instrument "Il Cannone" (the Cannon) on account of its powerful sound. He owned many other violins of the highest quality, but *Il Cannone* remained his lifelong favorite instrument.

Paganini preferred the thinnest possible strings made to his exact specification. He used plain, unwound gut E, A, and D strings and wound gut G strings. These thin strings responded to the slightest touch of the bow, making possible the most beautiful dulcet tone as well as complex harmonics. Paganini regularly tuned his strings up a half step and occasionally the G string up a minor third to B-flat to increase the brilliance of the instrument.

To facilitate playing in the highest register of the instrument, the neck was reset at a steeper angle and the original fingerboard was lengthened and replaced with ebony wood. He used a low bridge to effortlessly play the highest notes. In addition, the bass bar was replaced with a longer and stronger piece of wood so the belly of the instrument could support the increased pressure caused by higher tuning. Many of these changes were universally adopted, and by the middle of the 19th century, virtually every old violin was converted to these new standards.

In the early part of his career, Paganini played transitional bows. Later, he switched to a modern bow made by Jacob Eury, one the greatest early French bow makers. In spite of his fondness for this bow, he experimented with many other bows including the metal bow invented by J.B. Vuillaume.

Since Paganini did not use either chinrest or pad, he supported the violin to a great extent with his left hand, the scroll in front of his face, the instrument tilted from the G toward the E string's side at a 45-degree angle and his left elbow firmly planted to his chest.

Paganini held the bow between the thumb and the nail digits of his fingers, about an inch above the frog. His right elbow was in the immediate vicinity of his hip, with his upper arm barely participating in the execution of bow strokes. He negotiated string crossings by rotating his upper arm, barely raising his elbow.

Paganini's Caprices contain a whole arsenal of bowings—spiccato, sautillé arpeggio, saltando, staccato volant, rapid string crossing, brisure* of slurred as well as separate bows, up and down bow chords, chords in the middle of a slur and on the string staccato.

The left hand challenges include scales, arpeggios on the entire length of the fingerboard, every conceivable double stop combination, chords, and unusual stretches. **

---

*Brisure is bowing alternately on two nonadjacent strings in rapid succession. (See Caprice #2 bars 29-31)

**Paganini was an excellent guitar player and he used a common guitar technique. Reaching with his index finger, he played the low note with the left side of the nail digit. (See Caprice 1 bar 22 and caprice #3 bar 56.)

Some of the Caprices were probably created as early as 1801, but not published until 1820 after Paganini sold the manuscript of his Caprices to the Italian music publisher Ricordi in 1817. The original manuscript in three volumes contained six, six and twelve Caprices, respectively. Paganini did not proofread the publication. Therefore, the first edition is full of mistakes, including wrong notes, rhythms, dynamics and tempo markings. A second edition, again without the composer's proofreading, is the source of a slew of new misprints. There are approximately 50 editions, copies or near copies based on previous editions. Finally, in 1974 Paganini's manuscript was published.

This Urtext Edition is based on this manuscript, the only one known of the Caprices. Obvious slips of the quill by the composer are corrected in the text. If clear intentions of the composer could not be ascertained, the questionable note is printed in parenthesis.

The 24 Caprices by Paganini are the ultimate challenges for virtuoso violinists. They have no equal "either in beauty, originality or difficulty of performance," remarked the great violinist Ole Bull.

The Caprices have been sources of inspiration for many great composers such as Schumann, Liszt, Brahms, Rachmaninoff, Lutoslawski, Dallapicola and others, writing transcriptions, arrangements and sets of variations using Paganini's themes.

Leopold Auer was among the first of the great pedagogues to espouse the Caprices for his most advanced students. Auer was the teacher of some of the 20th century's greatest violinists; Elman, Zimbalist and of course, Jascha Heifetz, who became "the father of modern violin playing," to quote Itzhak Perlman. During Heifetz' long career, he performed many of Paganini's works, including the Caprices. Indeed, the Caprices were core material in his Master Classes. He himself, even well past age 70, was in full command of every aspect of violin playing. His mastery of the music, spotless intonation, riveting performance style and his interpretive genius remained intact to the end of his life. He played and taught the Caprices, freely sharing his mastery and pedagogical wisdom and was always ready to encourage, explain and demonstrate the right performance style.

Jascha Heifetz' fingerings and bowings as well as his performance suggestions are integral parts of this edition.

ENDRE GRANAT

CAPRICE No. 24 by Niccolo Paganini, excerpt from composer's manuscript

CONTENTS

24 Caprices

NICCOLO PAGANINI, Op. 1
edited by Endre Granat

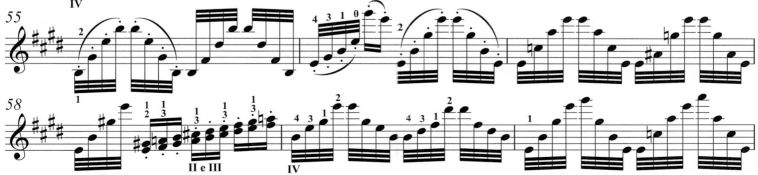

Moderato

2

Sostenuto

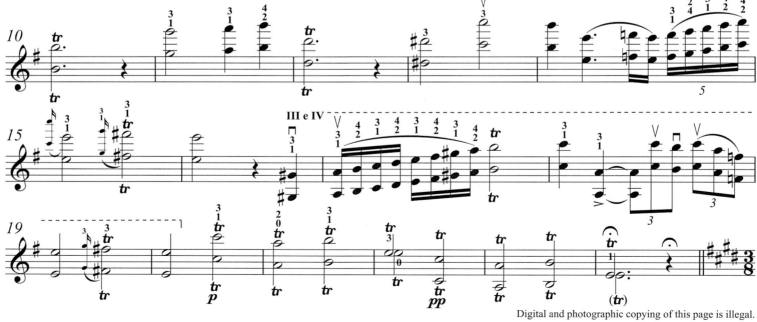

Sostenuto

Maestoso

4

14

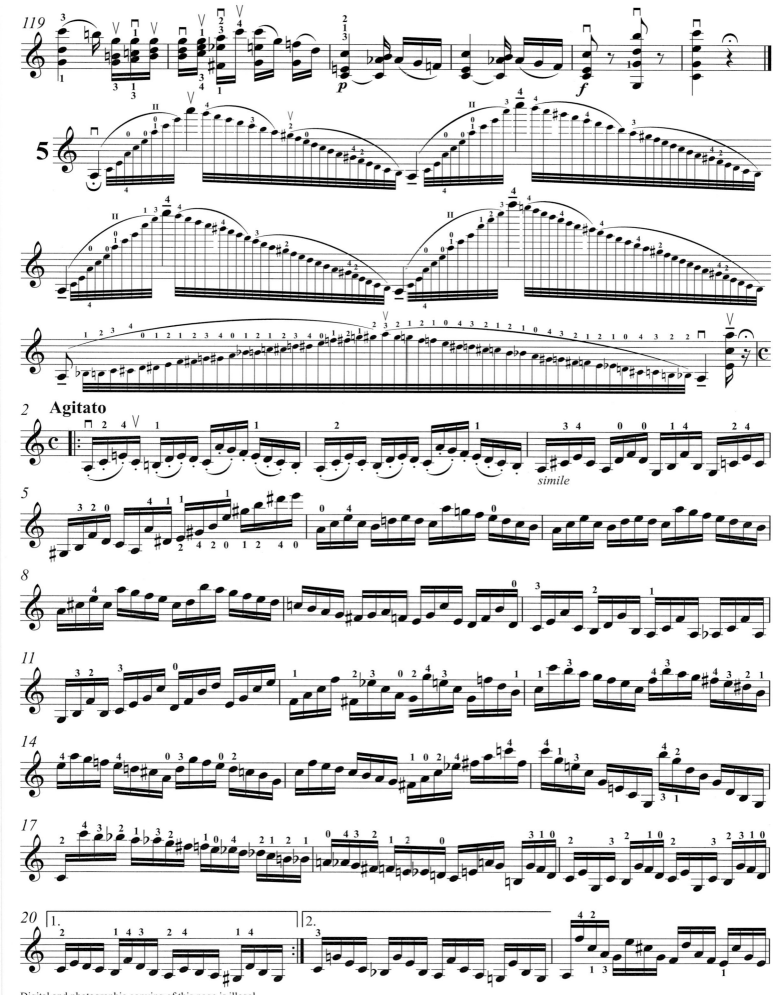

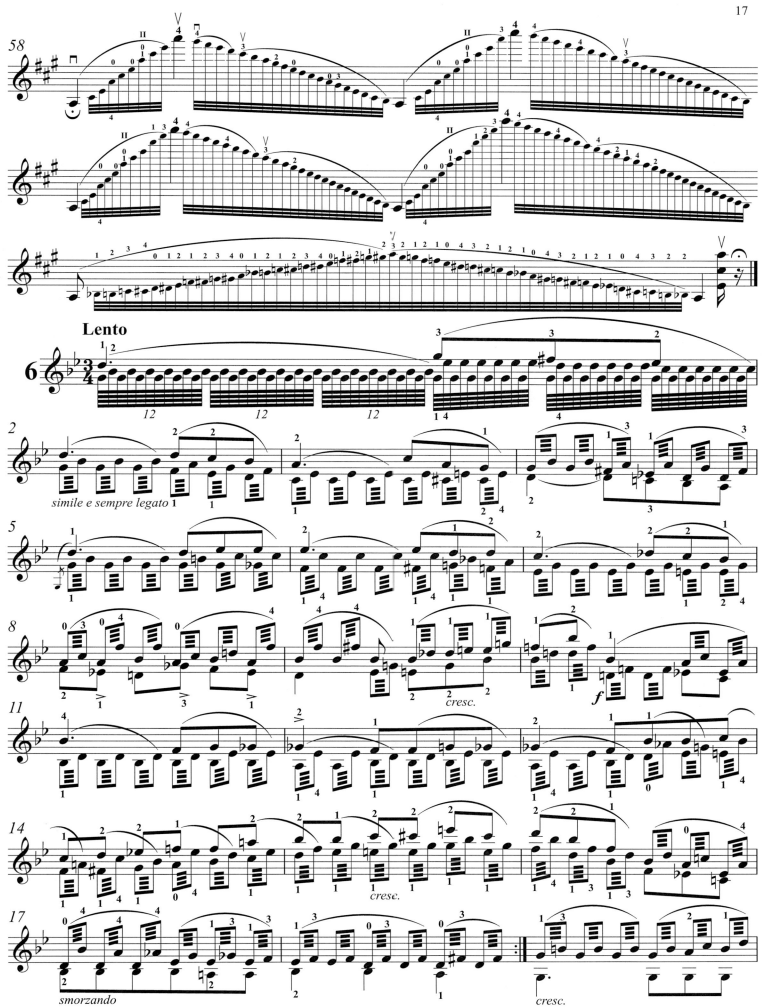

Lento

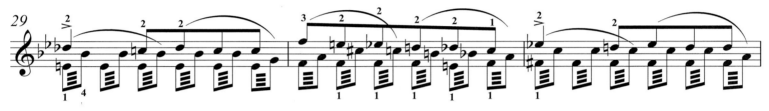

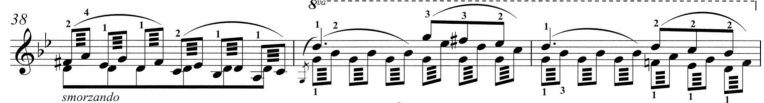

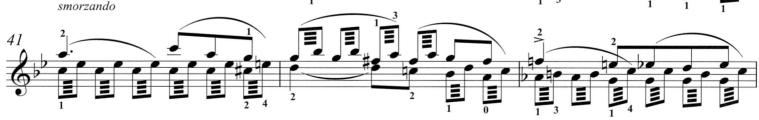

20

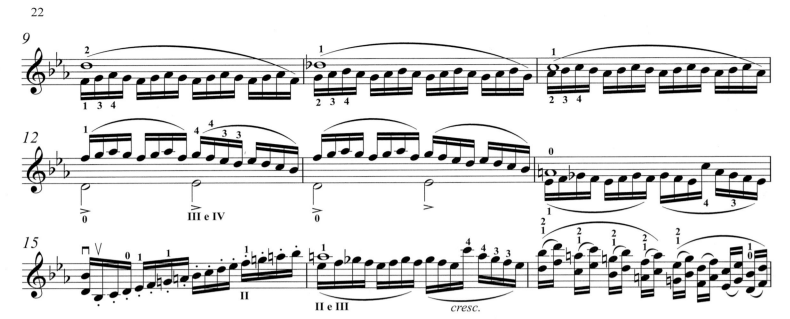

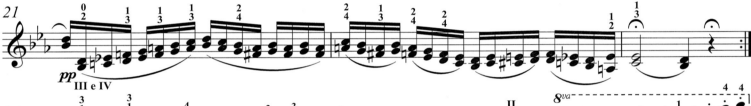

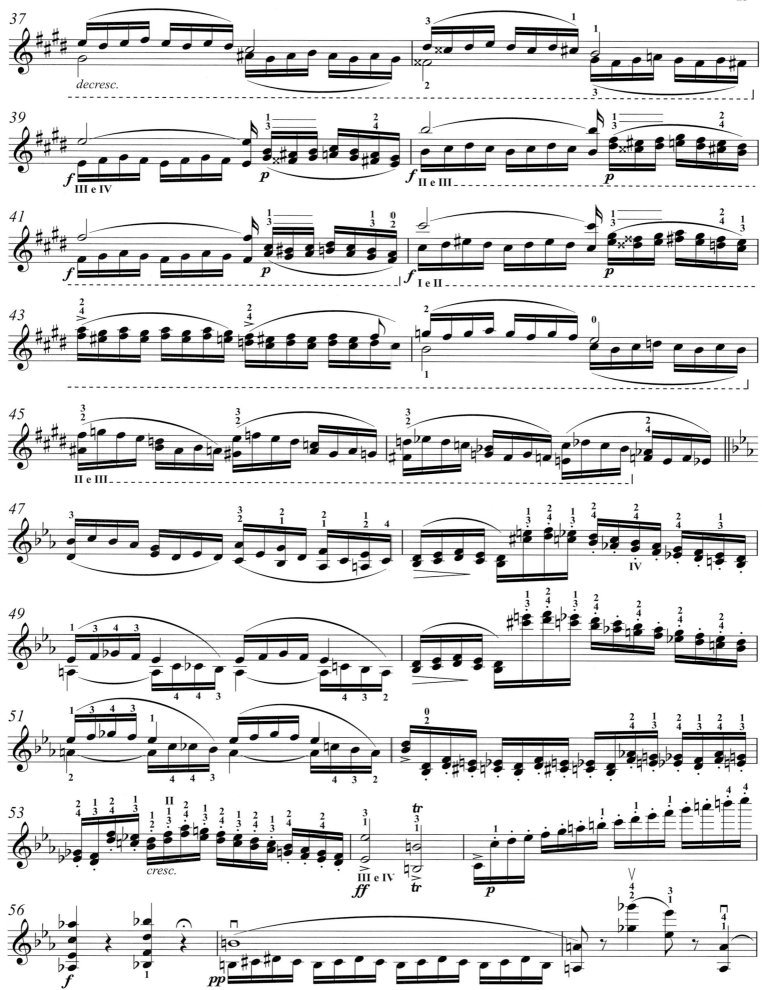

24

Allegretto

sulla tastiera imitando il flauto

imitando il corno sulla 3 e 4 corda

Andante

11

Presto

Tempo primo

Allegro

D.C. senza replica al Fine

Moderato

14

simile

simile

cresc.

15

Posato

Fine

D.C. al Fine

39

Minore

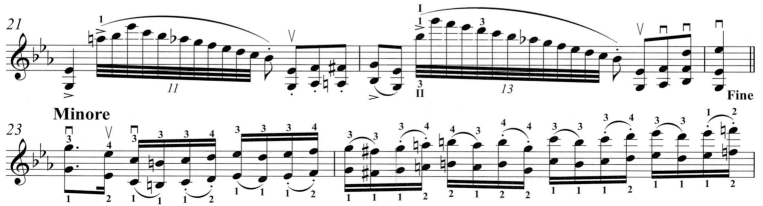

Corrente

Tutta sulla IVª corda

18

Allegro

Fine

D.S. senza replica al Fine

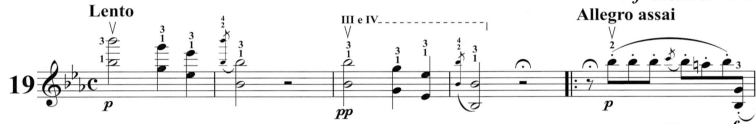

Lento   III e IV------------   **Allegro assai**

19

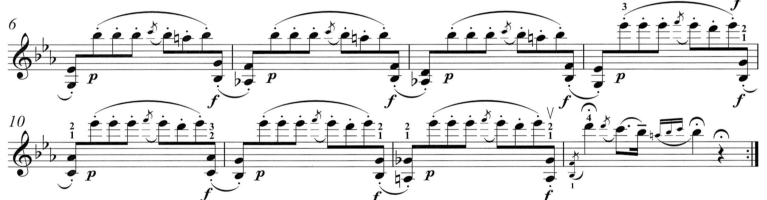

Minore

Tutta sempre IVᵃ corda

f la prima volta e p la seconda

44

Amoroso

D.C. al Fine

21

con espressione

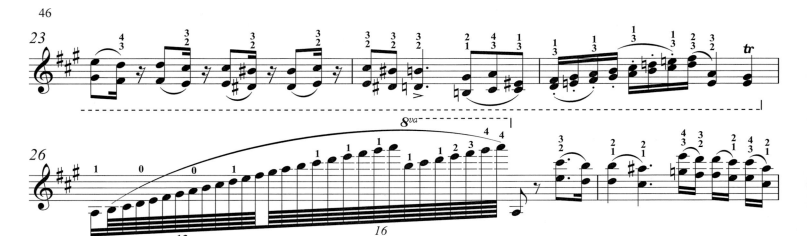

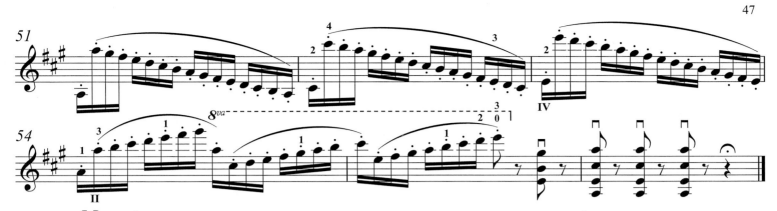

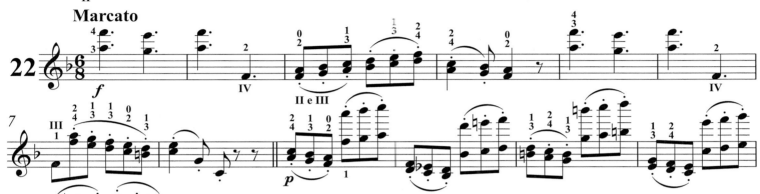

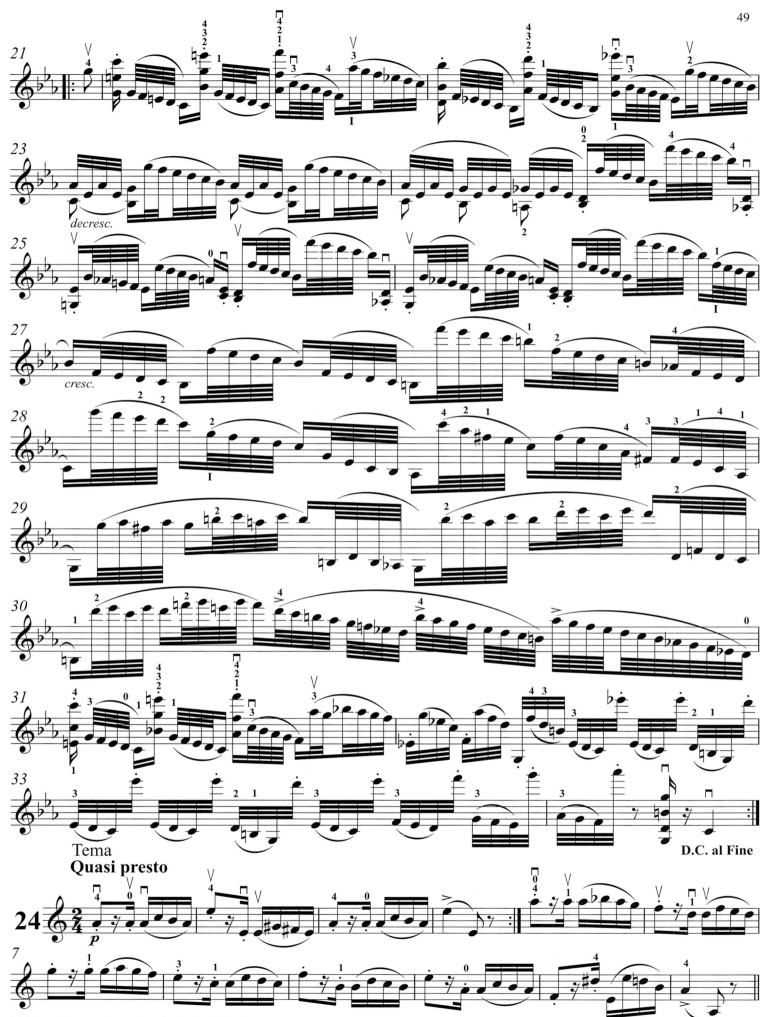

Tema
Quasi presto

24

D.C. al Fine

Var. 10

Var. 11

Finale